Capillary Phenomena And Supercooling

Edward August Rykenboer

In the interest of creating a more extensive selection of rare historical book reprints, we have chosen to reproduce this title even though it may possibly have occasional imperfections such as missing and blurred pages, missing text, poor pictures, markings, dark backgrounds and other reproduction issues beyond our control. Because this work is culturally important, we have made it available as a part of our commitment to protecting, preserving and promoting the world's literature. Thank you for your understanding.

Capillary Phenomena and Supercooling

A DISSERTATION

SUBMITTED IN PARTIAL FULFILLMENT OF THE REQUIREMENTS
FOR THE DEGREE OF DOCTOR OF PHILOSOPHY IN
THE UNIVERSITY OF MICHIGAN

BY

EDWARD A. RYKENBOER

EASTON, PA.:
ESCHENBACH PRINTING CO.
1917

TABLE OF CONTENTS.

Acknowledgment.. 4

Part I.

Supercooling in Capillary Tubes:
    Introduction 5
    Discussion of Supercooling.................................... 6
    Subject of Investigation...................................... 14
    Method and Apparatus... 15
    Results 21
    Interpretation of Results.................................... 26

Influence of Variation in Experimental Method:
    Variation in Rate of Cooling................................. 29
    Variation in the Material of Which the Tube Is Made.......... 30

Part II.

Effect upon the Supercooling of the Molecular Aggregation of the Material in the Liquid State:
    Introduction... 32
    Chemistry of Molten Sulphur.................................. 33
    Influence of Foreign Material upon the Formation of Crystallization Nuclei.. 35
    Method and Results... 36
    Interpretation of Results.................................... 41

Conclusions 43

ACKNOWLEDGMENT.

To Professor S. Lawrence Bigelow, for his instruction and guidance throughout this investigation and for his helpful criticism of the dissertation, sincere thanks are offered by the author.

To Professor Edward H. Kraus, for his interest in the dissertation and for class-room instruction, thanks are also due.

The author also wishes to express his appreciation to Professors William D. Henderson, Floyd E. Bartell, Harrison McAllister Randall, Walter F. Hunt and Dr. James E. Harris, for their instruction and suggestions in both class-room and laboratory.

CAPILLARY PHENOMENA AND SUPERCOOLING[1]

PART I—SUPERCOOLING IN CAPILLARY TUBES

Introduction

In mountainous regions the existence, at a definite altitude, of a clearly marked "tree line," indicates that above this the average temperature is too low for the trees to withstand. Certain forms of vegetation cannot survive the winter above certain latitudes. It would appear to be a logical conclusion that the completeness with which all moisture within the tree or plant is frozen is at least one factor determining whether it lives or dies.

Under certain conditions liquids may be supercooled many degrees below their freezing points without solidification. It occurred to us that sufficient smallness of cells or capillary tubes might make possible a degree of supercooling such that at least some of the contained moisture did not freeze and that this might be the reason that some plants or trees were not "winter killed," but resumed their growth in the spring. In winter, trees and plants are frequently subjected to temperatures below the freezing point of the dilute solutions in their cells and pores. Trees give off moisture in winter at low temperatures and the amounts given off are more than can be explained by the vaporization of the ice present in the tree as a result of freezing, which indicates that there must be some circulation of liquids, though this may be small in amount. That the contents of the larger vessels freeze solid is doubtless true but whether the contents of the very minute ones freeze also is not so certain. If they do not, they could furnish the small amount of circulation which appears to be maintained. When different specimens of a single variety of tree growing at different altitudes are compared, it is found

---

[1] Contribution from the Chemical Laboratory of the University of Michigan.

that the capillary tubes become progressively smaller as the height at which the tree grows is increased. This seems to point to a natural fortification against the lower temperatures experienced at high altitudes. At any one altitude the pores in the summer wood are smaller than those formed in spring, but since the year's growth is very small this would not necessarily indicate that the smaller tubes were formed later in the season as a preparation for winter. We were unable to find any exact data bearing on these points, indeed we did not find any reference to the considerations just outlined, in our examination of the literature, either botanical, physico-chemical or physical.

Furthermore, the question of pore size as determining, if it does determine, the degrees of supercooling possible without solidification, may be significant in connection with cold storage. For it is well known that many food products, after being frozen and then thawed, are less palatable. Possibly for each substance there is a temperature, below which it should not be brought.

The subject seemed to us of interest amply sufficient to justify a careful study of the amount of supercooling obtainable in capillary tubes and we hoped we might possibly succeed in formulating the degree of supercooling as a function of the diameter of the tube.

Discussion of Supercooling

The literature upon the subject of supercooling in capillary tubes is very meagre and is confined practically to a single contribution by H. C. Sorby.[1] He made a brief study of the temperatures at which water froze in capillary tubes of different diameters. He did this because he observed that in quartz cavities, liquids, that he supposed to be water, remained in the fluid state far below the freezing point of water. In tubes from 1/4 to 1/40 of an inch in diameter the freezing point was found to be about —6° C, in tubes smaller than 1/40 of an inch he found he could carry the super-

---

[1] Phil. Mag., [4] 18, 105 (1859).

cooling much further and in tubes of a diameter varying from 1/200 to 1/300 of an inch water froze at —17° C. On the other hand he found that there was no decided difference in the point at which freezing occurred in tubes varying from 1/200 to 1/700 of an inch nor in tubes with diameters from 1/4 to 1/40 of an inch. However, while the values for the tubes included in each of these ranges were the same, the two sets of readings were different. No conclusions were arrived at nor was any explanation offered for the phenomenon.

Van der Mensbrugghe[1] refers to supercooling in capillary tubes, among a number of other facts, which he uses as examples to demonstrate the application of a formula derived from thermodynamical considerations. The formula follows:

$$K = \frac{k - AtS \frac{d^2T}{dt^2}}{VX}$$

K = specific heat.
k = specific heat if surface has no potential energy.
A = thermal equivalent of the unit of work.
t = absolute temperature.
S = free surface.
T = potential energy of surface of contact (of a solid and a liquid which wets it).
V = volume.
X = specific gravity of the liquid.

The exact form of the function which expresses T by means of t for any liquid whatever is not known, but for a given liquid, the values of the coefficients of an equation such as $T = \alpha + \beta t + \gamma t^2 + \ldots$ can be obtained. According to Van der Mensbrugghe the values of β and γ for water are very small, and permit the powers of t higher than the second to be neglected. For the same liquid $\frac{d^2T}{dt^2}$ is negative and from this it follows that the quantity of heat to be supplied or taken away from unit weight of water, to raise or lower the temperature one degree, in general increases with t and also with S. Consequently it will be necessary to supply or withdraw much more heat to raise or lower the temperature one

[1] Phil. Mag., (5) 2, 450 (1876); (5) 4, 40 (1877).

degree, if the total surface of a given mass is increased by any means, such as dividing it into many small spheres or introducing it into a capillary tube.[1]

In capillary tubes it is necessary to ascertain the sign $\frac{d^2T}{dt^2}$, in order to foresee the quantity of heat necessary for a variation of potential energy in the surface of contact between the liquid and walls. If the sign is negative, we must conclude that K increases with the surface S and consequently the smaller the tube diameter the larger will be the value of K. However, $\frac{d^2T}{dt^2}$ is a continuous function and for any decided difference in S/V there ought to be a corresponding difference in K, which would mean a difference in the supercooling, the other conditions remaining unchanged. A consideration of Sorby's results shows that this is not the case, since the diameters vary widely over ranges of equal supercooling values: the value S/V changing greatly with no corresponding change in supercooling. It seemed possible that Sorby's results were not accurate or that he had omitted to consider some important condition or source of error. But our experiments, described later, tend to confirm his results in this particular, and it becomes evident that the formula, as given, is of doubtful value, at least in its application to liquids in capillary tubes.

Although supercooling in capillary tubes has received so little attention, the general subject of supercooling and the conditions under which a supercooled liquid will crystallize

---

[1] The ratio S/V increases as the volume of the mass diminishes, and, consequently, since d^2T/dt^2 is negative, the smaller the diameter of the mass or drop the greater will be the value of K. Van der Mensbrugghe believes that this explains how M. Mousson (Bibl. Univ. de Genève, 3, 296 (1758)) was able at very low temperatures to keep drops of water of less than $1/2$ mm diameter in the liquid state, when disposed upon a surface which they did not wet. In the same way, Tomlinson (Students' Manual of Natural Philosophy, p. 553) could see minute drops of water, alcohol and ether roll upon the surface of a fixed oil raised to more than 200° C.

In this connection it can be shown that the sign d^2T/dt^2 changes under certain conditions: for water the change occurs in the vicinity of the maximum density.

spontaneously has been the subject of a good deal of study. Summarizing the results we may say that the spontaneous crystallization of a supercooled liquid depends upon two factors:

(a) On the spontaneous power of crystallization: this is determined, and can be measured, by the number of centers of crystallization which are formed per unit of time in unit mass of the liquid.

(b) On the velocity with which the boundary between liquid and crystal is shifted (i. e., velocity of crystallization).

Crystallization[1] in a supercooled liquid never occurs homogeneously throughout the whole mass of the liquid but always begins at certain points or centers of crystallization, the number of which depends upon the amount and duration of the supercooling and the volume of the supercooled mass. Crystal threads grow outwards from these centers and spherical crystal aggregates result. In many substances the number of centers can be determined by counting the spherical crystals, each crystal aggregate containing a center of crystallization. For this purpose the material, enclosed in a thin-walled glass tube, is heated just above the melting point and is then rapidly cooled 40° to 80°. Then the centers usually begin to appear. If they appear too slowly the tube can be warmed slightly and the number of centers will be increased; but the velocity of crystallization increases also, so that the whole mass tends to crystallize when the first center appears and the counting is soon ended. With increasing initial supercooling the number of centers formed per time and temperature unit increase at first to a maximum, but at temperatures about 100° below the melting point the number formed per unit time decreases rapidly. This behavior is well shown in the case of piperin as is manifest in the two tables following:[2] The amount of substance used in each case was 1/8 cc. The melting point of piperin is 129° C.

---

[1] Tamman: Zeit. phys. Chem., 25, 443 (1898).
[2] Tammann: Loc. cit.

TABLE I

Cooled quickly to $t°$ C	Time Minutes	No. of centers
35.1	2	0
	4	2
	8	3
	12	5
40.2	2	4
	4	10
	8	19
	12	23
45.1	2	1
	4	3
	8	5
	12	7

TABLE II

$t°$	No. of centers	
25.2	38	32
30.1	73	62
35.2	102	96
40.1	132	141
45.2	106	111
50.2	92	96
55.3	85	88
60.1	52	43
65.2	27	24
70.2	8	7
75.1	0	1

In Table II the number of centers given is in every case the number which appeared in exactly two minutes.

Table III shows the relation between the volume of the liquid and the number of crystal nuclei.

TABLE III

t	Cylinder I 0.25 cc	Cylinder II 0.5 cc	Cylinder III 1.2 cc
0	1	1	18
20	4	5	58
40	39	50	148
60	6	8	76

Capillary Phenomena and Supercooling

TABLE III—(Continued)

Cylinder	Lg. cm	Outer diam. cm	Thickness of wall cm	Volume cc
I	26.0	0.11	0.02	0.25
II	23.0	0.18	0.02	0.50
III	4.2	0.53	0.04	1.20

Figure I shows the graphical representation of the values given in Table III.[1]

The most significant facts brought out by this figure are that the number of crystal nuclei is not proportional to the volume of the containing cylinder and that the maximum value for each curve comes at the same point on the temperature axis. In general, however, the number of centers is greater, the greater the volume of the liquid, as would naturally be expected.

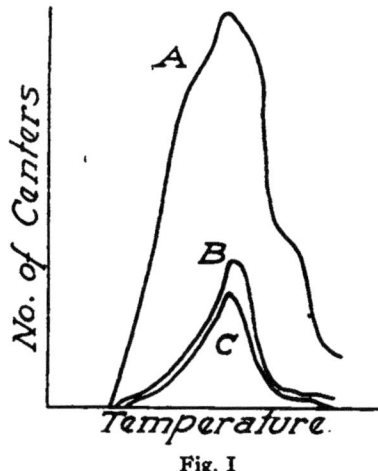

Fig. I

The second determining factor in the spontaneous crystallization of a supercooled liquid is the velocity of crystallization, or the speed with which the boundary between liquid and crystal is shifted. If the velocity is very small, centers might appear but they could not grow and the liquid would not crystallize. Piperin, for example, can be melted, then cooled until several centers appear and then if the temperature is lowered rapidly the centers remain the same size, and will not change until the temperature is again increased to a region where the velocity of cystallization is noticeable. To determine the velocity, the molten liquid is supercooled in a U-tube and inoculated at one end with a crystal nucleus. As time passes the crystal surface can be seen to grow. If

---

[1] Tammann: Loc. cit.

crystallization velocity is plotted against temperature a diagram will be obtained similar to Figure II.[1]

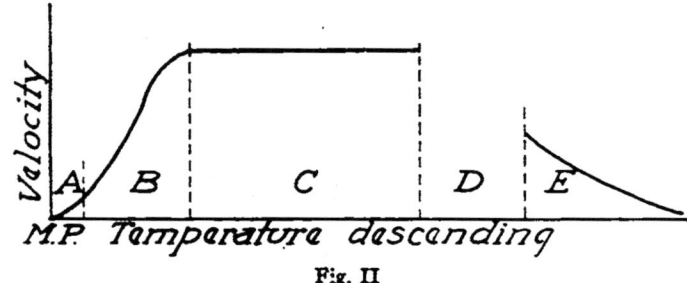

Fig. II

In considering this diagram three things must be borne in mind: (1) Bath temperatures are represented on the horizontal axis. (2) The temperature at the boundary layer between crystal and liquid is not the temperature of the bath, on account of the heat of crystallization. (3) When layers of liquid relatively far from the boundary layer are heated to the melting point, due to heat of crystallization, the velocity is high. If a thin layer only is heated to the melting point, the velocity will have a constant value as long as the heat of crystallization is sufficient to maintain this temperature in a thin layer. As the temperature at the boundary falls the velocity decreases still further.

At first, in range A, as the temperature of the bath is lowered, the values for velocity are small. The reason for this is that, owing to the insufficiently rapid removal of heat or crystallization, layers of liquid adjacent to the crystallizing boundary are heated to temperatures even above the melting point and the penetration of the crystal nuclei into these layers is retarded. In range B the velocity increases, in spite of the fact that the bath temperature is lower, since the heat of crystallization is sufficient to cause layers, that are far from the crystallizing layer, to be heated to the melting point. As the temperature of the bath decreases still further in range C, only enough heat is furnished to establish the melting

---

[1] Tammann: Zeit. Elektrochemie, 10, 532 (1904).

point temperature in a thin layer. If the maximum velocity is less than 3 mm per minute, the heat liberated per unit of time is usually not sufficient to maintain the temperature of the melting point constantly at the boundary for an extended fall of temperature in the bath, and, in consequence, range C shrinks to a point. Furthermore, with substances showing a rather high velocity the heat liberated will heat layers of liquid, still farther from the crystallizing boundary, as in range B, and the curve will continue to rise beyond C into range D. In this range the velocity will rise to its maximum value. Finally, in range E the heat of crystallization is no longer sufficient to establish the melting point temperature even in a thin layer, and the velocity decreases with increasing supercooling.

The viscosity is also related to the spontaneous power of crystallization and to the velocity, and its relation is brought out by the curves in Figure III.[1]

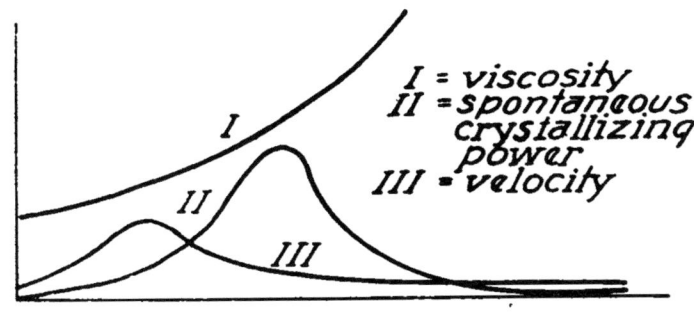

Fig. III

The viscosity of the liquid increases with descending temperature and frequently, in a small range of temperature, passes through all values from those of a syrupy liquid to those of a solid mass, and if the temperature is still further lowered the mass becomes hard and brittle. After passing the temperature range in which the maximum number of centers of crystallization are formed, the viscosity becomes very large and few, if any, centers appear in the brittle, glassy

---

[1] Tammann: Loc. cit.

mass. If centers did form they would not grow on account of the very small values of crystallization velocity in this region and the substance becomes highly stable, since the number of centers of crystallization is a measure of the instability of a supercooled liquid. The more there are, the greater is the tendency of the liquid to change its state of aggregation. A liquid can therefore be the more easily undercooled the fewer the nuclei in it, and the more slowly these nuclei grow.

Subject of Investigation

We undertook to ascertain experimentally the maximum degrees of supercooling obtainable in glass tubes with diameters varying from about one-half a centimeter down to the smallest we could conveniently manipulate. Our purpose was to settle the question as to whether supercooling could be more easily produced and could be carried further in capillary tubes than in larger tubes. Our hope was to find and establish some mathematical relation between the maximum supercooling effect and the diameter of the tube. And our intention was to include a number of different substances in the investigation.

At first the experiments were confined to a study of water as the supercooled liquid. Mixtures of ice and salt were employed as cooling agents, but they proved to be a source of annoyance due to the fact that the apparatus soon became encrusted with a layer of salt, which made it practically impossible to take readings on the thermometer immersed with the supercooled tubes. Solutions of solid carbon dioxide in ether or in alcohol were also used, as was a current of carbon dioxide gas escaping from a pressure tank and therefore cold, due to the expansion. The solutions, of course, evaporated rapidly and it became evident that the quantities we should have to use would involve too great a cost. We therefore abandoned, for the time at least, our originally planned work on water, and solutions in water, and turned our attention to materials whose melting points were between 100° and 125°. With these, all the cooling that was needed was obtained by allowing the temperature of the bath containing the experimental tubes to fall gradually to that of the room. Almost all of the work was done with sulphur, oxalic acid, orthoacettoluid, β-naphthol and acetanilide. These substances were chosen because, with the exception of oxalic acid, they do not decompose at temperatures near their melting points.

Method and Apparatus

The material, enclosed in glass tubes immersed in a bath, was first heated to a temperature a few degrees above its melting point. It was held at this point until all had melted; the temperature was then allowed to fall and the temperature at which crystallization began in each tube was noted.

Along with each series of capillary tubes was included one large or standard tube. This tube was of sufficient diameter so that the enclosed mass represented a volume so large that the number of nuclei formed was considerable and the tube gave the smallest possible values for supercooling. This condition was fulfilled by tubes having diameters from 4 to 5 mm, which was smaller than we had anticipated. Numerous larger tubes were tried but none of them gave supercooling values different from those obtained with the 4 to 5 mm tubes. We then fixed, as it were, the upper limit above which the effects we were studying were not to be expected. Tubes of this dimension we called our standard or comparison tubes.

Ordinary soft glass tubing was steamed well to get rid of any soluble material and then left standing for several hours filled with the usual potassium bichromate-sulphuric acid cleaning mixture. It was then washed with distilled water, dried by drawing through it a current of air, and drawn down to the capillary sizes desired in the blast lamp. Suitable lengths of the capillary were then cut off with a small flame, thus sealing both ends. These little tubes were left sealed until we were ready to fill a series and start a set of observations. In filling the tubes the substance to be used was heated just above its melting point and held there until the whole mass had melted. The tubes selected were opened, warmed and their ends were dipped into the liquid where they filled by capillary ascension. They were then removed and the substance, still liquid, was drawn up by suction into the tube far enough to allow the end to be sealed. The tubes were then reheated to a few degrees above the melting point of the substance in a bath and any leak could be detected by the ascension of bath liquid in that tube. Ordinarily, the length of the column of substance was only a few millimeters.

In order to regulate the rate of cooling, and in order to have normally a rather slow rate of cooling, it was found necessary to use a bath of from 600 cc to 800 cc capacity. A large beaker answered our purpose and an inner bath served to keep the temperature more nearly uniform for all the tubes contained within it. A variety of different liquids were tried in the bath but sulphuric acid was finally chosen in spite of certain risks of accidents thus entailed. The great advantage of sulphuric acid was that it could be used over a large range of temperature, but after repeated heatings it was found that it was satisfactory only for temperatures below 225 degrees. The bath was placed upon sand and an ordinary Bunsen burner was used for the heating.

After experimenting with several methods of stirring, a device was finally adopted which consisted of an inner bath of glass, a tube 3 cm in diameter and 22 cm long, closed at the lower end. The upper end projected through the center of a horizontal wooden wheel to which it was firmly attached. This wheel was supported on ball bearings and was rotated by an electric motor. Projecting almost to the bottom of the inner bath was a small glass tube which had attached to it, two platinum carriages. The capillary tubes, usually three or four in number, projected through openings in these carriages and were fastened at the top to the glass tube by means of an ordinary rubber band. The glass tube was fastened to a separate support and being stationary, while the inner bath was rotated, the arrangement effected the stirring.

A thermometer extended through the glass tube and its

mercury bulb was at the same level in the bath as the material enclosed in the capillary and standard tubes. The thermometers, ten inches long, were made especially for this work and have a scale about five inches in length on the lower half, while the upper half is left blank for purposes of fastening in position. In this way the whole scale was immersed in the liquid of the bath and no correction was necessary. While this was not

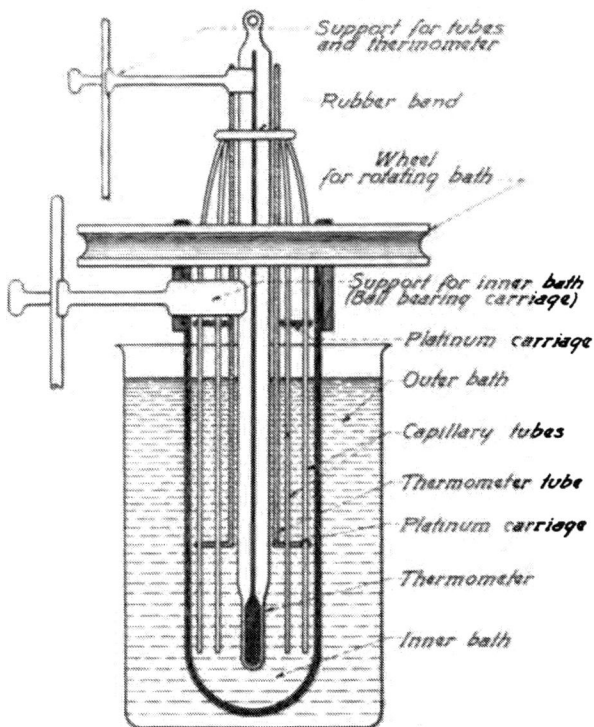

Fig. IV

important, the readings were much more easily followed where the whole scale was visible. The scales were made in seventy-five degree lengths and each succeeding thermometer overlapped the one before by twenty-five degrees. The thermometer, being removable, permitted the use of a wide range in temperature because one thermometer could be taken out and another covering a different range could be inserted.

The arrangement of tubes and thermometer is shown in Figure IV.

It was necessary to have an adjustable means for regulating the rate of cooling of the outside bath. A cooling coil of water was out of the question, since the cold coil, immersed in the acid at perhaps two hundred degrees, might break and under these conditions, explosions and serious accidents might result. A cooling coil of sulphuric acid was tried but was not found to be very efficient unless of a size so large that it would interfere with the readings. Finally a satisfactory method was devised by means of which cold sulphuric acid was added while the hot acid was simultaneously drawn off, thus keeping the bath at a constant level. By means of a suction flask and pump connected with a two-liter bottle, the hot acid was drawn through a glass tube at the top of the bath, passed through condensers for the purpose of cooling it and then was allowed to fall into a bottle. At the same time, by means of a pressure flask, cold acid was forced into the bath from a reservoir immersed in running water. For most substances this cooling was sufficient, but in cases where the substance had a low melting point it was necessary to keep the reservoir surrounded with a mixture of salt and ice. These two outfits were so connected that by turning several valves the cooled acid was drawn over into the reservoir and the process was ready to be repeated. Though the apparatus looked, and was, rather complicated it was very quickly and easily set in action or stopped. Figure V shows the arrangement.

In carrying out the experimental part of the work it was necessary first, to select a thermometer such that the melting point of the material enclosed in the tubes came near the top of its scale. Then supercooling values could be read on the same thermometer. In some cases the supercooling was so great that, in spite of this precaution, another thermometer covering a lower range had to be substituted later. The thermometer and tubes were adjusted as previously described and the temperature was gradually raised to a point not more

Capillary Phenomena and Supercooling

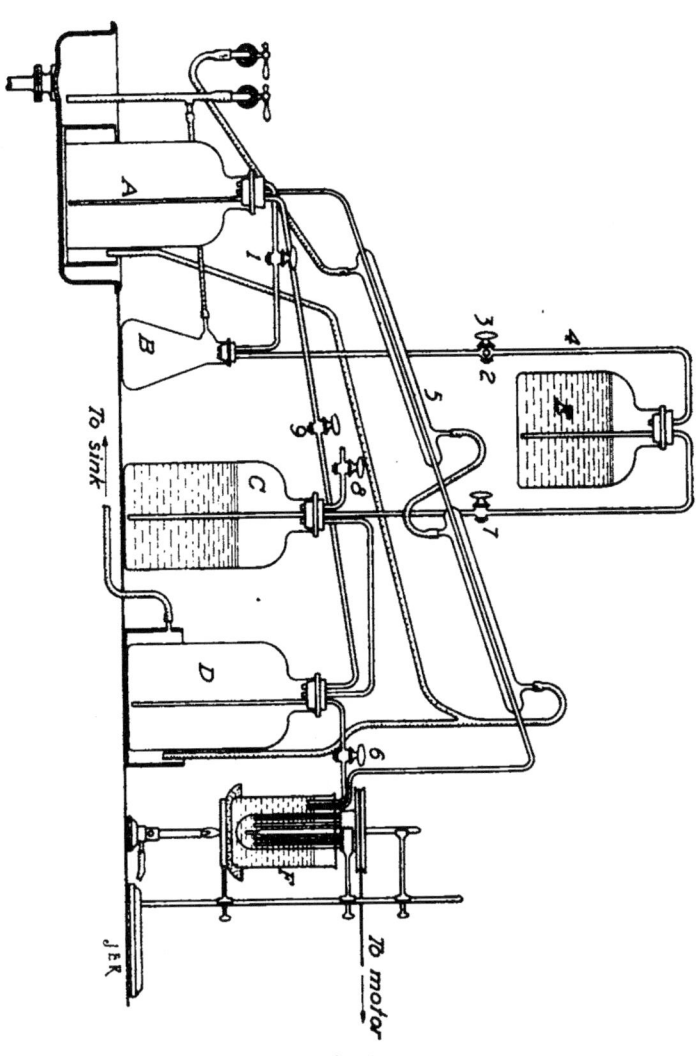

Fig. V

To Cool Bath: Open cock 1, close 9 and turn the three-way cock 3, closing it to 5 and leaving it open from 2 to 4. Then the suction of the water pump draws the acid from the bath F through the condensers into the cooling bottle A. At the same time leave cocks 6 and 7 open with 8 closed and water from reservoir E flows into pressure bottle C and causes the acid in D to pass through cock 6 into the bath.

To bring apparatus back to the original conditions: Close 1, turn cock 3 so that 4 is open to 5, close cock 6, open 9, open 7 leaving 8 closed and suction draws the acid back into D and at the same time draws the water from C into E. Cock 8 is to relieve the partial vacuum in C after the process is completed.

than five degrees above the melting point of the substance under investigation. With rapid heating the temperature of the inner bath lagged behind that of the outer bath, so, as the temperature of the outer bath approached the melting point, the rate of heating was gradually decreased. In this way it was possible to keep the temperature of heating from going more than five degrees above the melting point. The heating burner was then removed and the bath allowed to stand until the temperature had dropped several degrees. The cooling arrangement was then used to bring the bath down almost to the temperature which had been found by previous experiments to be the point where the material in the standard tube solidified. The bath was then allowed to cool more slowly, subject only to the cooler temperature of the room. A four-inch reading glass was used to magnify the smaller tubes so that the formation of the first nucleus could be noticed more readily. Immediately that this was seen, the temperature was read from the thermometer within the inner bath. The liquid of the bath also magnified the tubes within so there was no difficulty in making the required observation even with the smallest capillaries used. There was also no difficulty in noting when solidification began, since the transparent contents of a tube immediately became opaque, due to the solidified material enclosed. This procedure was repeated several times for each set of tubes and successive values of supercooling were obtained. After such a series of readings had been obtained the tubes were removed from the bath. The length of the column of confined material was then measured to tenths of a millimeter and the diameter in millimeters to three decimal places. The diameter was obtained by breaking the tube at a point where the material was enclosed and then inserting a short section of the tube vertically in a small clamp attached to a metal object plate. This plate was then put on the stage of a microscope and the inner diameter of the tube was measured by means of a calibrated scale in the ocular. A micrometer attachment allowed a hair to be moved across the field from one side of the tube to the other, the

Capillary Phenomena and Supercooling

movement being read directly by means of a calibrated drum on the ocular. The number of divisions on the drum multiplied by their actual value for the objective used gave the results in millimeters. Several readings were taken, as the cross sections of the tubes were not perfectly circular, and the mean value was recorded.

Results

The tables following give results obtained with some of the materials used. The data for all of our materials are not given, nor are all the data for a single substance shown. It is unnecessary to give more than we have given, since all results obtained were similar to those recorded. By degrees of supercooling is meant the temperature at which the first crystallization was observed, counting downward from the melting point of the substance. For instance, with sulphur, crystallization was first noted in tube 41 at 92° C. Then 114 — 92 = 22 degrees of supercooling.

The tubes are arranged in the tables in the order of increasing mean diameter. In all tables Lg. Col. = Length of

TABLE IV
Sulphur M. P. = 114–115° C

Tube No.	Mean Diam. in mm	Lg. Col. in mm	S. C. 1	S. C. 2	S. C. 3	S. C. 4	S. C. 5	S. C. 6
30	0.164	7.0	49.0	49.5	56.5	59.1	—	—
29	0.187	5.5	44.5	51.5	44.4	57.0	56.5	56.0
25	0.227	5.6	52.2	62.5	62.2	62.0	61.7	61.6
32	0.233	11.5	55.5	58.8	58.5	52.4	61.6	54.4
28	0.260	4.5	41.0	60.4	55.6	56.2	56.7	58.2
31	0.312	4.2	53.8	54.5	65.5	57.6	61.2	66.5
44	0.318	5.4	43.0	43.8	44.2	47.3	44.7	42.7
35	0.319	5.7	48.8	57.2	57.0	51.5	63.2	60.2
26	0.389	5.5	46.3	52.0	55.5	64.8	60.5	60.0
24	0.402	7.0	53.5	56.2	42.2	—	—	—
27	0.434	6.5	43.2	47.3	39.2	40.2	50.5	39.7
45	0.544	6.4	38.2	38.0	42.0	45.5	41.0	40.8
61	4.1	4.5	30.4	31.0	27.5	28.5	30.0	—
41	4.5	3.5	22.0	20.8	26.5	24.2	24.8	27.0

Column of material enclosed in tube; Mean Diam. = Mean Diameter of tubes; S. C. = Degrees of Supercooling; S. C. 1, S. C. 2, etc., represent values for successive heatings and coolings. Table IV contains some of the results obtained with sulphur.

TABLE V
Orthoacettoluid. M. P. = 110° C

Tube No.	Mean Diam. in mm	Lg. Col. in mm	S. C. 1	S. C. 2	S. C. 3	S. C. 4	S. C. 5	S. C. 6
69	0.209	5.0	37.0	34.8	36.4	35.0	36.0	39.6
77	0.223	—	38.7	35.5	—	—	—	—
68	0.291	4.4	29.2	29.8	31.5	33.1	33.5	32.2
67	0.401	5.1	30.5	30.5	30.9	32.9	33.0	32.9
72	0.471	—	29.5	33.9	29.9	33.5	33.6	—
66	0.530	3.2	29.3	30.8	31.0	32.0	33.8	33.5
65	0.568	5.1	31.6	32.1	33.7	35.7	34.8	35.4
71	0.727	—	34.5	31.7	31.2	33.5	34.9	—
64	4.0	4.5	23.0	23.5	22.5	24.2	24.2	25.0
70	4.0	—	19.6	23.8	24.0	18.6	24.2	—

64 and 70 were the standard tubes.

TABLE VI
β-Naphthol. M. P. = 122° C

Tube No.	Mean Diam. in mm	Lg. Col. in mm	S. C. 1	S. C. 2	S. C. 3	S. C. 4	S. C. 5	S. C. 6
80	0.327	4.2	16.8	18.0	17.0	16.6	17.8	19.2
91	0.342	5.1	11.8	13.3	16.2	13.2	—	—
83	0.353	4.0	14.7	16.0	14.1	17.5	18.2	17.4
79	0.382	4.0	14.5	15.0	16.7	16.7	18.5	16.0
82	0.394	5.0	10.5	16.4	13.0	16.3	18.6	17.3
90	0.409	9.5	14.0	13.2	16.0	16.0	—	—
81	0.420	11.0	13.0	13.0	14.5	16.2	16.2	16.3
89	0.459	5.2	15.8	15.7	18.3	16.7	—	—
88	0.499	4.1	15.7	15.6	16.1	16.3	—	—
87	0.672	2.5	14.7	14.0	15.5	16.8	—	—
86	0.695	3.2	15.3	18.4	17.5	17.5	—	—
85	4.3	4.1	6.5	5.6	5.4	6.0	—	—
84	4.3	4.0	5.5	4.5	4.5	4.5	5.2	5.5

84 and 85 were the standard tubes.

41 and 61 were the standard tubes and it can be seen that the supercooling was much less than with the capillary tubes. 35 and 44 were practically the same in size and yet there was a decided difference in the results. In this short table it looks as though 27 and 45, the largest of the capillary tubes, gave supercoolings that were consistently less than those of the smaller tubes, but these were exceptional cases, and later it will be seen that very small tubes give supercoolings no greater than those given by tubes of this size or even larger.

Table IV shows that it was impossible to obtain the same results in successive observations. This is equally true

TABLE VII
Acetanilide. M. P. = 114° C

Tube No.	Mean Diam. in mm	Lg. Col. in mm	S. C. 1	S. C. 2	S. C. 3	S. C. 4	S. C. 5	S. C. 6
131	0.174	5.6	46.6	47.8	42.5	47.3	—	—
123	0.182	5.5	48.0	48.0	—	—	—	—
129	0.189	6.5	47.6	46.7	47.2	47.0	—	—
130	0.203	4.5	47.7	46.7	46.8	47.4	—	—
126	0.206	7.2	47.7	47.4	46.6	45.6	—	—
128	0.213	5.4	45.3	47.5	46.8	46.9	—	—
132	0.234	4.4	46.6	40.5	43.6	44.6	—	—
127	0.248	4.5	45.2	46.5	45.8	45.3	—	—
120	0.249	2.4	47.0	47.7	—	—	—	—
121	0.249	5.8	47.6	43.7	—	—	—	—
122	0.264	4.3	46.9	46.0	—	—	—	—
125	0.285	1.8	47.6	47.5	46.5	45.2	—	—
117	0.328	5.1	46.0	45.4	—	—	—	—
114	0.433	3.3	42.9	45.3	45.1	45.6	44.7	—
118	0.336	3.2	46.8	47.6	—	—	—	—
119	0.336	4.0	45.0	46.0	—	—	—	—
116	0.353	4.5	46.1	45.5	—	—	—	—
113	0.405	3.1	44.7	46.0	45.0	45.0	46.0	—
112	0.409	4.0	44.0	45.2	43.9	44.1	44.6	—
110	0.466	2.5	43.8	45.3	45.1	44.7	46.0	—
108	0.575	5.1	43.1	43.1	43.6	44.2	44.0	—
111	0.677	1.8	—	43.0	41.0	41.9	43.4	—
109	0.698	4.5	38.7	38.7	39.8	42.0	38.8	—
115	4.3	5.0	37.5	37.5	—	—	—	—
124	4.8	6.5	36.7	33.0	36.4	38.4	—	—

115 and 124 were the standard tubes.

for the tables to follow. In some cases differences were very slight, but in many instances they were large. It is notoriously difficult to get concordant results upon supercooling, and bearing this in mind, it may be conceded, at least by those who have ever tried such experiments, that the results check better than might have been expected.

Here, although there was a wide range of tube diameter, the readings were almost the same in value. The smallest tubes gave, in some cases, equal supercooling or even smaller supercooling than the largest tubes, and we naturally expect them to give uniformly higher values in all cases. Here, also, a capillary tube 109 gave the same reading as the standard tube 124.

TABLE VIII

Oxalic Acid. M. P. = 98° C

Tube No.	Mean Diam. in mm	Lg. Col. in mm	S. C. 1	S. C. 2	S. C. 3
145	0.191	—	17.5	19.0	17.5
148	0.192	—	19.5	23.5	17.0
150	0.195	—	16.0	15.3	22.2
147	0.210	—	19.4	15.0	21.5
149	0.219	—	15.5	16.5	20.5
101	0.238	1.5	19.4	24.1	—
146	0.242	—	15.0	14.5	15.0
151	0.253	—	10.5	10.8	16.5
100	0.278	1.6	15.9	—	—
143	0.339	4.0	—	17.0	17.0
96	0.352	2.6	15.5	9.2	—
97	0.376	1.1	16.6	11.2	—
155	0.461	6.0	9.6	9.0	10.0
98	0.475	3.4	12.5	13.0	—
99	0.508	1.7	20.3	17.6	—
156	0.585	8.5	7.0	11.0	8.0
95	0.589	4.4	14.0	11.0	—
154	0.739	6.6	3.5	3.6	16.0
94	0.755	4.5	16.0	12.9	—
142	4.1	8.0	3.5	3.5	7.5
93	4.2	4.8	5.5	8.0	—

93 and 142 were the standard tubes.

Where the length of the column is not given it is because the thread of substance itself was broken into small segments due to the repeated heating. A column of from 4 mm to 6 mm in length sometimes broke up into as many as a dozen parts. This might have been caused by a slight decomposition of the acid as this splitting up was most pronounced with oxalic acid which loses its water of hydration just above its melting point. The substance was heated to only a few degrees above its melting point, just enough to make sure that all the material had melted. Sometimes the different fragments solidified at different temperatures, but usually they all crystallized out at the same time.

Here, again, some of the larger capillaries gave S. C. values almost as small as those found in the standard tubes 93 and 142. In tubes 145 to 151 columns of acid crystallized out at different temperatures, and on reheating these columns broke into a number of smaller segments, yet the results do not indicate that this further subdivision had much if any effect on the amount of supercooling. In some cases the readings were even higher than before, but as a rule the small segments gave values of supercooling practically the same as that obtained with the original column of material.

From a consideration of Tables IV to IX it is seen that, with very few exceptions, the contents of a standard tube solidified at a temperature above that at which the contents of the capillary tubes solidified. The difference, as a rule, was considerable, but comparing the results with the capillary tubes with each other, the amount of supercooling was not always the same for tubes of equal diameter, even when the length of the column was the same. The readings of the standard tubes did not always agree, but the differences here were much smaller than the difference between the results obtained in the capillary tubes. It is also evident that tubes of widely different diameters, but within what we may call capillary dimensions, gave practically the same readings. Comparing the capillary tubes with the standard tubes it is seen that the increase in supercooling is not proportional to

Table IX
Benzoic Acid. M. P. = 121.4° C

Tube No.	Mean Diam. in mm	Lg. Col. in mm	S. C. 1	S. C. 2	S. C. 3	S. C. 4	S. C. 5
174	0.132	5.3	25.2	36.9	43.4	—	—
164	0.152	2.0	—	41.6	49.0	48.4	49.9
161	0.167	6.6	26.4	46.6	41.3	41.4	41.4
175	0.170	2.5	26.0	21.6	19.0	—	—
176	0.179	0.8	39.9	21.3	13.4	—	—
163	0.192	5.2	15.9	19.4	18.4	18.4	19.4
168	0.217	6.5	22.2	31.4	14.9	—	—
173	0.235	7.0	32.8	23.1	38.4	—	—
178	0.262	7.5	19.4	27.9	32.4	—	—
177	0.265	—	40.6	32.9	24.4	—	—
172	0.276	2.6	27.2	35.4	32.9	—	—
162	0.281	6.0	28.2	28.1	32.3	32.4	32.4
170	0.308	7.3	24.4	30.4	24.4	—	—
165	0.311	4.3	—	31.2	29.9	37.4	23.1
169	0.339	2.6	30.9	34.8	35.0	—	—
160	0.354	6.8	22.6	41.4	36.9	32.9	41.9
171	0.453	2.6	37.4	35.2	20.9	—	—
167	0.458	2.3	47.9	33.4	36.4	—	—
179	0.459	2.2	44.2	32.9	28.4	—	—
159	0.459	11.2	10.6	37.4	37.4	32.3	39.6
158	0.894	3.5	21.2	31.4	41.4	45.9	16.4
157	4.1	2.5	9.3	16.6	12.4	16.4	13.4
166	4.4	2.4	7.6	8.9	8.9	—	—

157 and 166 were the standard tubes.

the decrease in diameter. It is also noticeable that the supercooling is independent of the length of the enclosed column of material.

Interpretation of Results

It is reasonable to suppose that the arrangement of molecules making up a crystal nucleus is characteristic for every substance and that some internal molecular configuration or rearrangement is necessary in order that a nucleus may form. It may be some such arrangement of the liquid molecules as given by A. Johnson[1] reasoning from the work of Laue and the Braggs on crystal structure. According to

---

[1] Phys. Zeit., 16, 269 (1915).

them, a crystal must have minimal symmetry; *i. e.*, must have one and only one of the 230 Schoenflies space groups, and at the same time it must conform with one of the 32 groups of symmetry. There must be some definite arrangement of the liquid molecules or atoms which, when the proper conditions are present, give rise to a crystal nucleus or center of crystallization. Now as the temperature of the substance is lowered below the melting point, crystallization takes place, but in materials such as we studied, the velocity of crystallization is such that the whole mass solidifies rapidly as soon as a single center appears. So when crystallization occurred in one of our tubes it denoted the temperature at which such a center first appeared. The molecules are in continuous motion within the liquid and no doubt many times assume the arrangement necessary for the formation of a center, but with small supercooling the viscosity is not great enough to retard the motion of the molecules and hold them in that position long enough for the centers to form and to allow the crystallization to begin. As the temperature decreases the viscosity is increased, thereby increasing the probability of crystallization until a maximum of probability is reached. Beyond this point the increased viscosity retards the formation of the centers or is so great that the internal rearrangement is hindered. Then if the temperature could be lowered enough without having a center form, the substance could be obtained in the form of a glass.

The number of centers formed spontaneously depends to a large extent upon the volume of the substance considered, and also upon the inclination of the curve obtained by plotting the number of crystal centers on one axis and the corresponding temperature on the other. See Figure VI.

If the number of centers increases rapidly with a decrease in temperature the conditions would be represented by curve X, but if the number of centers increases slowly with a decrease in temperature, curve Y would represent the conditions. Curve X could also represent the number of centers formed in a large volume, then curve Y would represent the conditions in a small volume of the same substance. Since in a large volume of a supercooled liquid the number of centers of crystallization formed at any given temperature is greater than in a small volume of the same material, the probability of a single center being formed at the given temperature will be greater in the large volume than in the small one. That is to say, if, in a certain volume there appeared four centers of crystallization and in a smaller volume only one appeared, the probability of just one center forming would be four times as great in the larger volume. Let a point where such a center appears be represented by A and A_1 on the curves in Figure VI. It is seen that the number of centers formed at this temperature is about four times greater in the case of curve X, or large

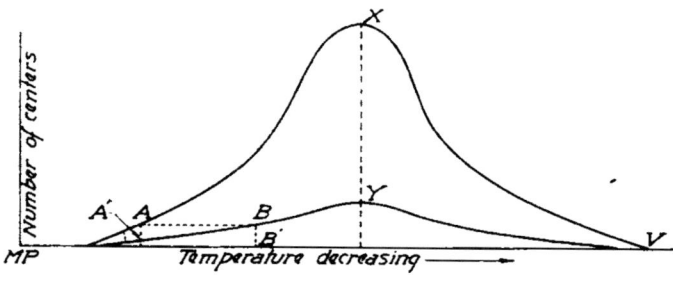

Fig. VI

volume curve, than for curve Y or curve of smaller volume. In order to have equal probability for both cases it would be necessary to pass along curve Y to point B. Point B represents the same number of centers as point A, and hence the probability of a single center forming would be the same. But point B is at a much lower temperature than point A and consequently, since all the materials used crystallized at the appearance of the first center, the supercooling in the case of the small volume would be much greater. If the volume became very small the probability might become so small that not even one center would even appear and in this case the liquid would remain uncrystallized.

If, in the cases cited above, the number of centers was very small even in a large volume, the temperature might be lowered several degrees beyond the temperature indicated by the probability factor before crystallization would take place, or in other words, before a center would appear. The actual appearance of a center might then, as it were, lag behind the temperature at which we would expect it to appear. In a small volume, such as is represented by a capillary tube, the temperature might even be lowered ten or fifteen degrees beyond the point indicated by the probability value, before the material would solidify. This would allow a series of small, though unequal volumes, to give values of supercooling distributed all through this temperature interval and explains, perhaps, the range of equal readings obtained with capillary tubes of different diameters.

The fact that the supercooling was not proportional to the decrease in tube diameter, is in agreement with Tammann's observation, that the decrease in the number of crystal nuclei was much greater than the diminution in volume seemed to warrant, and it supports the connection that we have attempted to establish between the supercooling and the number of crystal nuclei.

That the supercooling was apparently independent of the length of the enclosed column of material seems to indicate that perhaps it is the shape of the supercooled volume and not the actual volume itself that is the determining factor. Perhaps the arrangement of the imaginary units of volume with respect to each other tends to aid or retard the formation of crystal nuclei. It is conceivable that a crystal nucleus, to form and to grow, needs to have some definite quantity of the substance all around it. Then for any volume, a spherical shape would give the largest number of possible centers, and any other would give fewer. In the discussion above then, perhaps the cross section of the various tubes should be considered rather than the corresponding volumes.

INFLUENCE OF VARIATION IN EXPERIMENTAL METHOD
Variation in Rate of Cooling

The number of crystal nuclei formed in a given mass is dependent upon the time, and from the relation established between the number of crystal nuclei and supercooling (see Figure VI) we would expect to get greater supercooling under conditions of more rapid cooling. We found, however, that the rate of cooling made very little difference in the amount of supercooling obtained, as can be seen from the values given in Table X.

TABLE X
Sulphur M. P. = 114–115° C

Tube No.	Mean Diam. in mm	Lg. Col. in mm	S. C. 1	S. C. 2	S. C. 3	S. C. 4	S. C. 5
61	4.10	4.5	32.5	31.5	27.9	28.0	27.7
62	0.917	6.0	45.0	43.0	45.5	53.3	48.5
63	0.214	6.5	50.8	52.0	52.5	54.0	53.6
Heated to			140°	140°	140°	140°	140°
Rate of Cooling			slow	slow	fast	fast	fast
61	4.10	4.5	34.5	36.2	41.0	36.5	47.0
62	0.917	6.0	49.5	55.8	46.5	46.5	52.5
63	0.214	6.5	58.9	61.7	66.0	61.4	62.0
Heated to			155°	155°	170°	170°	170°
Rate of Cooling			fast	slow	slow	slow	fast

Fast Cooling = about 5° per minute.
Slow Cooling = about 5° in 10 minutes.

The rate of cooling is not constant. At higher temperatures it is more rapid than at lower temperatures but the mean values above are close enough. The difference in supercooling under the different conditions of cooling from any one temperature was no greater than the difference in consecutive readings under the same cooling conditions.

Variation in the Material of Which the Tube Is Made

The point of solidification is mainly a function of the material itself, but there is a possibility of other factors influencing the crystallization to a certain extent. For example, different supercooling values might be obtained in tubes of glass and of platinum or contact with different substances might help or hinder supercooling. Some experiments were carried out to test this possibility, using acetanilide as the supercooled material. Two glass tubes of exactly the same diameter and from the same piece of tubing, containing acetanilide, were heated in the ordinary manner and the solidifying point was noted. This was repeated several times in order to increase the reliability of our conclusions. Strands of glass and platinum were made of nearly the same diameter. The columns of acetanilide in the capillaries had been made of the same length. A piece of the glass thread was put in one tube and a piece of the platinum thread was put in the other, and they were long enough to pass through the acetanilide. The heating and cooling was then repeated in exactly the same way as before, both tubes being allowed to cool at the same rate.

TABLE XI
Acetanilide   M. P. = 112° C.   Heated to 120° C

Tube No.	Mean Diam. in mm	Lg. Col. in mm	Sub. Added	S. C. 1	S. C. 2	S. C. 3	S. C. 4
X	0.411	—	—	45.4	42.0	45.7	—
Y	0.411	—	—	45.3	45.2	44.8	—
X	0.411	5.2	Platinum	41.0	43.6	42.1	41.5
Y	0.411	5.2	Glass	41.7	44.8	44.0	43.5

Diameter of Strands—Platinum = 0.121 mm. Glass = 0.116 mm.

The slight difference noted in the supercooling with the threads was practically the same as the difference between the successive readings of the tubes without them. These experiments led us to conclude that the nature of the surface in contact with the crystallizing liquid does not influence the temperature at which crystallization begins.

That a difference in the surface tension between the large and small tubes would account for the difference in supercooling hardly seems plausible since the difference in surface tension must be very slight. G. Quincke's[1] experiments seem to show that the difference between the surface tensions in tubes of different diameters is slight and that the surface tension is greater in larger tubes. The experiments

---
[1] Wied. Ann., 52, 1–22 (1894).

of P. Volkmann,[1] however, indicate that the surface tension is smaller in larger tubes, but his experiments also show only slight differences between the surface tension values.

If in the tubes there were any relation between the surface tension and the supercooling obtainable, there ought to be some relation between the position of the center of crystallization and the surface. No such relationship could be found, the contents of the tubes beginning to solidify at times in the interior and at other times, perhaps, in the surface layer. If a change in the surface tension changed the amount of supercooling obtainable, it would be reasonable to expect a gradual, continuous change in the amount of the supercooling, increasing or decreasing as the diameters of the capillaries were varied. No evidence of this sort is perceptible in any of the tables. Some of the capillary tubes gave nearly the same values of supercooling as the standard tubes, while others of almost the same size gave much greater values.

PART II—EFFECT UPON THE SUPERCOOLING OF THE MOLECULAR AGGREGATION OF THE MATERIAL IN THE LIQUID STATE

Introduction

Since we believe that the formation of a crystal nucleus is due to a definite molecular configuration within the liquid, we would naturally expect to have a change in the character and number of nuclei if the molecular arrangement in the liquid were changed. This would undoubtedly involve a change in the supercooling values also. In fact, we could detect such a change in the liquid by observing changes in the values of supercooling. Such a transformation or rearrangement could be brought about in several ways but we shall confine ourselves to a study of the effect of variation in the temperature to which the material is heated. Sulphur has proved itself to be an ideal substance for this purpose and a review of the changes brought about in the liquid sulphur

---

[1] Wied. Ann., **53** 633–663, 664–666 (1894).

by changes in temperature is necessary before our experimental results can be interpreted.

Chemistry of Molten Sulphur

The effect of the temperature to which liquid sulphur has been heated, has been the subject of a large amount of work. D. Gernez[1], by making use of the inoculation method for determining the freezing point, found that the freezing point of sulphur is not constant, but depends upon the temperature to which it has been heated. He found that when sulphur was fused at 121° C and cooled, the freezing point was 117.4°. When the liquid was heated to 144° it had a freezing point of 113.4° and when kept at 170° for five minutes the freezing point fell to 112.2°. Later he found[2] by heating sulphur to 160°, then allowing it to cool to 100° and holding it there for some time, that when the sides of the containing vessel were rubbed, a deposition of "pearly" sulphur was obtained. Smith and Carson[3] represented this pearly or nacreous formation by S_{III} orthorhombic by S_I and monoclinic by S_{II}. They found that the liquid from which the nacreous modification has been separated may be converted into monoclinic or orthorhombic sulphur by the touch of a corresponding crystal. In the conversion of liquid to ordinary crystals in this way, the reaction takes place with seven-fold rapidity after the nacreous crystals have been deposited, and Gernez considers that at the temperature of 169° the allotropic pearly modification is produced, and by its solution in the rest of the liquid the latter is in the condition of a supersaturated solution. F. W. Küster[4] found that the amount of insoluble sulphur present after solidification was dependent only upon the rate of crystallization and the temperature at which the crystallization occurred, and not upon the temperature to which it had been heated nor upon the length of time of heating. He concludes that the soluble and insoluble forms of

---

[1] Comptes rendus, 82, 1151 (1876); Phil. Mag., [5] 2, 79 (1876).
[2] Comptus rendus, 98, 144 (1884).
[3] Zeit. phys. Chem., 71, 661–676 (1911).
[4] Zeit. anorg. Chem., 18, 365 (1898).

sulphur are isomerides. Other experimenters, however, seem to agree that the insoluble variety of sulphur is present in increasing amounts as the temperature is raised above the melting point. P. Duhem[1] explains the difference in velocity of crystallization of sulphur as due to the difference in concentration of the insoluble form. Alexander Smith[2] found that the formation of insoluble sulphur takes place in an irregular manner as the temperature is raised above the melting point and that the depression of the freezing point is proportional to the amount of insoluble sulphur thus formed. In a later investigation[3] he found that yellow mobile sulphur (S_λ) predominates from the melting point to 160° and that the brown viscous or amorphous (insoluble) sulphur (S_μ) increases greatly in amount above 160° at the expense of S_λ. He thought that this indicated a transition point, since a separation into the two phases, yellow and brown liquid sulphur, was observed.[4] Later, however, he[5] accepted the view of Hoffman and Rothe[6] that there is no transition point in the ordinary sense, for if the rate of cooling was diminished the discontinuity did not appear and therefore the two modifications must, under ordinary conditions, be completely miscible with each other. The apparent separation into two phases was brought about by the differences in temperature which arise in a column of the liquid owing to the poor conduction of heat, in reality there being no formation of two phases, the difference in color being accounted for by the difference in temperature. Smits and Leuw[7] apparently accepted these views also since they found that the liquid sulphur contains the two forms S_λ and S_μ in equilibrium proportions.

---

[1] Zeit. phys. Chem., 23, 193–266 (1897).
[2] Ibid., 42, 469 (1903); Proc. Roy. Soc. Edin., 24, 299, 342 (1902).
[3] Proc. Roy. Soc. Edin., 25, 588 (1905).
[4] Jour. Am. Chem. Soc., 27, 797–820 (1905).
[5] Proc. Roy. Soc. Edin., 26, 352 (1906); Zeit. phys. Chem., 59, 448 (1907); Jour. Am. Chem. Soc., 29, 499 (1907).
[6] Zeit. phys. Chem., 55, 113–124 (1906).
[7] Proc. Akad. Wetensch. Amsterdam, 14, 461 (1911); Zeit. phys. Chem., 83, 221–241 (1913).

In addition to S_λ and S_μ, A. H. Aten[1] has described two other forms of sulphur, S_π and S_ϕ. S_ϕ is not formed, however, by the action of heat upon sulphur and is of no interest to us. S_π is formed when sulphur is heated above its melting point and then is rapidly cooled. The relative quantities of S_λ, S_μ and S_π present in sulphur which has been heated to various temperatures have been determined by Aten.[2] The amount of S_π is at a maximum when the sulphur has been heated to 180° and at this point the amount present is 6.5%. The quantity of S_μ increases as the temperature rises to 448° C, the greatest rate of increase being between 170° and 180°. S_λ decreases as the temperature increases. He gives the composition at 180° as $S_\pi = 6.5$ percent, $S_\mu = 20.4$ percent and $S_\lambda = 73.1$ percent.

Summarizing all this: when sulphur is heated to various temperatures above its melting point there are present principally the four modification S_γ, S_μ, S_π and S_{III}. S_λ is soluble sulphur and is present in the greatest amounts, decreasing, however, with increase of temperature above the melting point. S_μ is insoluble or amorphous sulphur which increases in amount as the temperature is raised with the maximum rate of increase between 170° C and 180°. S_π is present in small amounts but increases to a maximum as the temperature is raised to 180° and then decreases. S_{III} or pearly sulphur, begins to form at 160° C. The various forms of sulphur occurring together in the liquid state are mutually miscible.

Influence of Foreign Material upon the Formation of Crystallization Nuclei

Tammann[3] has observed that the addition of soluble materials to a supercooled liquid causes a decided change in the number of crystal centers and in the temperature at which a maximum number forms per unit time. By the addition of one substance the temperature for maximum number of

---

[1] Zeit. phys. Chem., 81, 257–280 (1912); 88, 321–379 (1914).
[2] Ibid., 86, 1–35 (1913).
[3] Ibid., 25 453 (1898).

centers was lowered while the addition of another substance would cause a shift towards higher temperatures. In some cases the maximum point was at the same temperature but the number of centers was changed, with some added materials the number being larger, and with others, it was smaller. Of course this caused a decided change in the slope of the curve. We have indicated the relation between the number of crystal nuclei and supercooling and have also shown the effect of the slope of the curve representing the variation in number of crystal centers with temperature. It would seem, then, that added foreign materials would cause a change in supercooling, either increasing it or decreasing it as the case may be.

As sulphur is heated to various temperatures above its melting point, increasing amounts of new and in that sense foreign materials are formed as has just been described, consequently a shifting of the curve representing the number of crystal nuclei could be expected. Since the amount of supercooling in capillary tubes depends upon the position of the maximum and the slope of the nuclei curve, any such shifting would be indicated by a change in the amount of supercooling obtained.

Method and Results

The degrees of supercooling of sulphur when cooled from temperatures just above its melting point have been given. When it was heated to points between 120° and 200°, changes in the supercooling values with the capillary tubes were observed. The heating was carried on in the usual way. Both rapid and slow cooling was tried with no noticeable difference in the results. Table XII shows the effect of heating to different temperatures upon the amount of supercooling afterward obtained, and it also shows that whether the cooling is fast or slow the results are practically the same.

In obtaining the results given in Table XII the tubes were first allowed to cool slowly from the temperature given in the table and then the time of cooling was shortened for the same tubes from the same temperature point. The fast cooling was about 12° per minute while the slow cooling

Table XII

Sulphur   M. P. = 114–115° C

Cool = Rate of Cooling   Heat = Temperature to which Substance was heated

Tube No.	Mean Diam. in mm	Lg. Col. in mm
61	4.10	4.5
62	0.917	6.0
63	0.214	6.5

Tube No.	S. C. 1	S. C. 2	S. C. 3	S. C. 4	S. C. 5
61	30.4	31.0	27.5	28.5	30.0
62	36.0	47.0	47.3	46.5	50.2
63	37.8	41.5	54.4	42.5	53.0
Cool	slow	slow	slow	slow	fast
Heat	125°	125°	125°	125°	125°
61	32.5	31.5	27.9	28.0	27.7
62	45.0	43.0	45.5	53.3	48.5
63	50.8	52.0	52.5	54.0	53.6
Cool	slow	slow	fast	fast	fast
Heat	140°	140°	140°	140°	140°
61	34.5	36.2			
62	49.5	55.8			
63	58.9	61.7			
Cool	fast	slow			
Heat	155°	155°			

Tube No.	S. C. 1	S. C. 2	S. C. 3	S. C. 4	S. C. 5	S. C. 6	S. C. 7	S. C. 8
61	34.0	34.5	37.0	43.5	44.2	42.0	46.0	44.5
62	45.5	44.5	45.5	51.0	50.5	45.5	50.5	56.0
63	93.0	92.5	80.0	66.0	86.0	80.0	76.0	80.0
Cool	slow	slow	slow	fast	fast	fast	fast	fast
Heat	170°	170°	170°	170°	170°	170°	170°	170°

Tube No.	S. C. 1	S. C. 2	Tube No.	S. C. 1	S. C. 2
61	38.3	41.0	61	33.5	42.0
62	48.0	48.0	62	48.0	56.2
63	75.0	75.5	63	59.5	66.2
Cool	slow	fast	Cool	slow	fast
Heat	190°	190°	Heat	225°	225°

Tube No.	S. C. 1	S. C. 2	Tube No.	S. C. 1
61	41.0	36.5	61	47.0
62	46.5	46.5	62	52.5
63	60.0	61.4	63	62.0
Cool	slow	slow	Cool	fast
Heat	170°	170°	Heat	225°

was about 1.2° to 2° per minute. This was repeated at each successive elevation of the temperature to which the heating was carried, but as can be seen from the table, no great change in the supercooling was observed. At about 170° a decided change was noticed in the readings with the smallest tube 63. The largest tube 61 did not show such a large change and the intermediate tube 62 gave values between those of the other two. Tubes of practically the same diameter gave wide variations, as subsequent data will show, but as a rule the values of supercooling were larger than those given by this tube 62. When the heating was carried to about 225°, smaller values were again obtained which persisted even when the tubes were reheated to 170°, the temperature corresponding to the maximum supercooling. It may be inferred that the modification which formed at 170° was permanent since a tube heated to that temperature and cooled gave the same value when reheated to 125° and cooled at the same rate.

With the ordinary supercooling of sulphur from its melting point the whole mass solidified in an instant as soon as the first center appeared, but where the supercooling was carried to room temperature before a center appeared the rate of crystallization was decidedly slow and the solidification of the mass continued to grow from the first center formed while the temperature was lowered perhaps ten degrees in five minutes. The fact that no more centers formed even when the tube was so slowly cooled through ten degrees, seems to point to a small number of centers even at the maximum point.

A graphical representation of the data in Table XII is given in Fig. VII. The horizontal axis represents the degrees of supercooling and the vertical axis shows the temperature to which the heating was carried before the supercooling was measured. Points on the curves represent average values. Although Curve B crosses Curve C at the lowest preheating temperature used, it is evident that it follows the contour of the curve for the standard tube for its whole length, and this might be expected since the tube is hardly of capillary diameter.

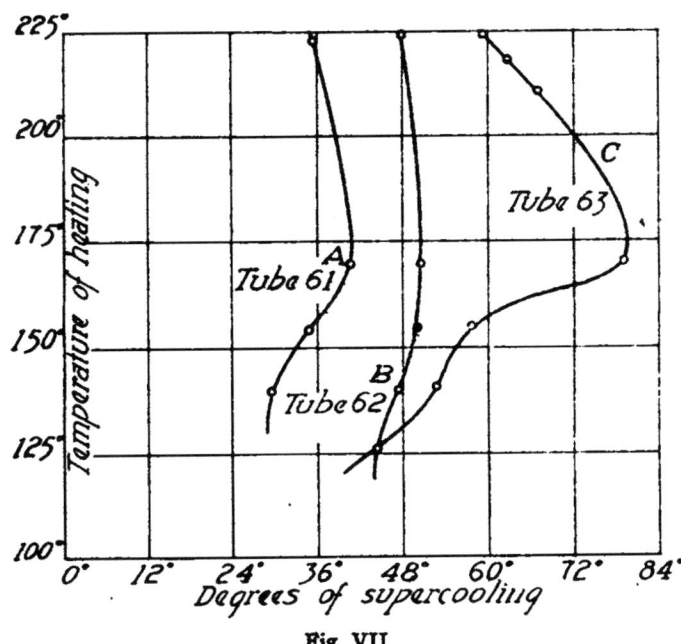

Fig. VII

In order to show that the change at 170° was permanent a series of capillary tubes were heated to 170°, then cooled to 100° and held there for five hours. The supercooling values were then determined and they corresponded to those obtained without this long wait, instead of to those obtained after heating only to a lower temperature. The tubes were again heated to 170° and this time cooled to 75° and held at this temperature for several hours. The results were similar to those obtained when the wait was at 100°. If the change within the liquid had not been permanent it would surely have reversed itself to at least some extent, during these long waits. The experimentally observed values are given in Table XIII.

TABLE XIII

Sulphur

Tube No.	Mean Diam. in mm	Lg. Col. in mm	S. C. 1	S. C. 2	S. C. 3	S. C. 4
219	0.191	5.6	55.0	64.0	51.0	58.7
222	0.205	4.3	55.5	87.5	83.0	78.5
218	0.211	4.2	43.8	70.0	72.5	73.7
217	0.237	5.2	44.0	88.0	71.0	75.9
214	0.252	5.5	44.0	59.4	59.0	56.3
213	0.267	5.7	59.0	83.0	81.0	79.0
215	0.271	6.5	53.0	64.5	76.5	77.5
216	0.276	5.2	48.0	78.5	70.5	71.0
212	0.321	3.9	41.0	48.5	70.8	74.0
211	0.339	4.8	47.0	56.0	58.0	55.0
210	0.429	3.5	50.7	—	71.0	69.0
Temp. heated to			125°	185°	185°	185°

After the readings S. C. 2 were taken, the sulphur was heated to 185°. It was then cooled to 100° and held at this point for five hours and then cooled as usual giving the readings in S. C. 3. This procedure was repeated for the values in the column headed S. C. 4 except that the temperature was first lowered to 75° and held here for five hours. It was then cooled as usual giving the readings in S. C. 4.

Table XIV gives more data of the same kind as that in Table XIII and confirms further our belief that holding the temperature constant at a point far below the temperature where we presume a permanent transformation took place, is without effect in reversing the transformation.

Table XIV
Sulphur

Tube No.	Mean Diam. in mm	Lg. Col. in mm	S. C. 1	S. C. 2	S. C. 3
206	0.201	4.7	84.5	91.0	100.0
201	0.220	5.6	68.5	58.0	55.0
205	0.238	5.8	68.0	82.5	81.5
204	0.272	3.5	69.0	83.0	89.2
203	0.281	4.0	88.5	74.0	95.5
202	0.284	4.0	59.0	64.0	82.0
198	0.470	8.2	68.0	64.5	73.0
199	0.655	5.4	67.0	62.0	60.0
Temp. heated to			190°	185°	185°

After the readings S. C. 2 were taken the sulphur was heated to 185°. It was then cooled to 100° and held at this point for three hours and then cooled as usual, giving the readings in S. C. 3.

Interpretation of Results

The greatly increased supercooling obtained with capillary tubes after heating to 170° or above indicates a broad shifting of the crystallization center curve towards lower temperatures. The probable change is indicated in Fig. VIII.

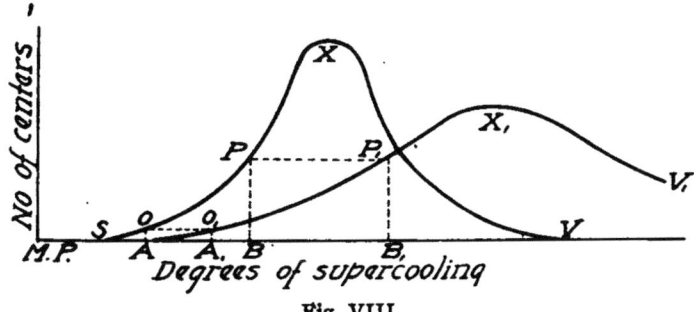

Fig. VIII

The effect of added materials upon the position and character of the nuclei curve has already been discussed. In Fig. VIII the added materials are the various forms of sulphur formed by the action of heat at temperatures above the melting point. Curve X represents the conditions in liquid

42   *Edward A. Rykenboer*

sulphur which has been heated only to the melting point and Curve X_1 represents conditions resulting from heating to 170° C. The two curves start to leave the horizontal axis at approximately the same point since the change in supercooling values for the standard tube is very small. As has been said, in a large volume such as in a standard tube, a center of crystallization will appear practically as soon as suitable conditions are present, and this would be where the curve starts to leave the temperature axis. The maximum value for Curve X_1 is below that for Curve X since we have found that the number of centers formed in sulphur that has been heated to 170° is smaller than when it is heated only to the melting point. The maximum point will also be farther along the temperature axis for Curve X_1 since the increase in supercooling for the capillary tubes is very large. With a lower maximum point shifted to the right, Curve X_1 will have a more gentle slope than Curve X.

The point of crystallization for the standard tubes is represented by O and O_1 the projections of which upon the horizontal axis give the temperature readings A and A_1. P represents the point where sulphur in a capillary tube, that has been heated only to the melting point, will crystallize out, the increased elevation of the point counterbalancing the decreased volume. Thus P and O would represent equal probability of crystallization. Point P_1 represents the crystallization point for the same tube after it has been heated to 170°. Equal elevation for the same volume indicates equal probability for the formation of a crystal nucleus. But in the case of P_1 the temperature is lower, which corresponds to greater supercooling.

Let us assume that S_μ and S_π have a combined effect in shifting the curve of crystal centers to the right in Fig. VIII. The increase in supercooling indicated by the gradual rise of Curve C in Fig. VII would then be attributed to the gradual formation of S_μ and S_π. In the neighborhood of 160° the rate of formation of S_μ suddenly increases and this is indicated by the bend in the curve at S continuing to V. The influence

Capillary Phenomena and Supercooling

of S_π now grows less since the maximum percentage comes at 170° and simultaneously S_{III} or nacreous sulphur is formed. If we assume that the addition of S_{III} to the fused mass causes the curve to shift in the same direction as does S_μ and S_π, then there will be no decided break in the curve but the curve will continue to rise more gradually to the right, the increasing amounts of S_{III} partially making up for the decreased rate of formation of S_μ and S_π. Apparently, however, S_{III} at temperatures above 170° exerts an opposite and stronger effect than does S_μ for there is a sharp bend in the curve at 170° and above this temperature it gradually approaches the vertical axis. The corresponding Curve A for the standard tube shows the same effect but less pronounced.

Conclusions

We have designed a form of apparatus for the measurement of supercooling in capillary tubes.

We have shown that decidedly greater supercooling can be produced in capillary tubes than in tubes of larger diameter.

We did not succeed in formulating a mathematical connection between the amount of supercooling obtainable and the diameter of the capillary.

We have developed a plausible explanation for the increase in supercooling found possible in capillary tubes.

We have obtained evidence indicating that the material of the tube has little if any effect on the degree of supercooling, and have reached the conclusion that small changes in surface tension are likewise of insignificant importance.

We have found that in the case of sulphur, the amount of supercooling depends upon the temperature to which the substance was heated previously.

We have offered a plausible explanation of this interesting phenomenon.

Printed by Libri Plureos GmbH in Hamburg, Germany